A note from the author

HELLO, I WANT TO FIRST TELL YOU HOW PROUD I AM OF YOU FOR INVESTING IN YOURSELF ON YOUR JOURNEY TO GROWTH AND SELF-IMPROVEMENT. I AM EXCITED FOR THE OPPORTUNITY TO SHARE THIS EXPERIENCE WITH YOU IN THE FORM OF FUN AND THOUGHT-PROVOKING MATERIAL. I HOPE THAT YOU EMBRACE THE EXPERIENCE OF EXPLORING YOURSELF AND ALLOW YOURSELF TO BE THE FOCUS. I HOPE THAT YOU EMBRACE THE EXPERIENCE OF EXPLORATION AND FOCUS ON YOURSELF.

HAVE AN AMAZING JOURNEY.

WITH ADMIRATION,

Dedication

I dedicate this book with love to my amazingly complex, thoughtful, nurturing, beautiful, compassionate, resilient black women. I created this to be both conversational and connected to us as Black women. Our village is fragile and vulnerable, considering the current landscape, we need each other more than ever. This serves as your opportunity to self-reflect, explore and grow into your new space. Hopefully, this opens an opportunity to ask questions you never have, say things you've kept quiet on, share compassion with your fellow black woman and take accountability for things you were afraid of. I believe in our power, humility, grace and patience. You got this sis!

The Baddie that owns
this journal is ...

INTRO

With this journal, I welcome you to the rest of your life. Our independent moments turn into the stories that make up who we are and how we lived. This journal provides prompts that serve as opportunities to expand your thinking. Challenge yourself to go there, live there, breathe there, create there, explore there, and come out on the other side. This is a book of love, light and destiny. We are in this together.

Love, peace and soul

RECOMMENDATION

THIS IS A JOURNAL OF FREEDOM AND AUTHENTICITY. GO IN WHATEVER ORDER YOU'D LIKE. SOME HAVE PROMPTS. OTHERS HAVE PROMPTS TO JUST WRITE WHAT'S ON YOUR HEART. ACTIVITIES ARE INCLUDED TO CHALLENGE YOU TO EXPAND YOUR HEALTHY ROUTINES. THIS IS A FEEL-GOOD SPACE FOR YOU TO EXPLORE YOURSELF AND SAFELY MAKE THE JOURNEY.

Identify The Feeling

FEELING CHART

Happy

Sad

Skressed

Confused

Chillin'

Embarrassed

Appreciated

Disappointed

Irritated

Scared

Angry

Pissed

My nerves bad

Sick & Tiyd

Silly

Hurt

Fearful

Insecure

Disgusted

Surprised

"FEELINGS RESULT FROM THOUGHTS. NOT THE OTHER WAY AROUND."

SHARDE' O.

LIST YOUR FAVORITE SONG ... WRITE ABOUT THE MEMORIES IT TRIGGERS FOR *you*

REMINDER

Dear self, change requires discomfort. Get used to it.

Write about how that statement on the previous page made you feel.

Date: - - - - - - -

Feeling of the day: - - - - - - -

To complete by: _____

BUCKETLIST

Stuff I am going to do:

WHAT HAVE YOU STRUGGLED WITH IN YOUR RELATIONSHIPS WITH YOUR PARENTS? YOU KNOW HOW THEY DO ... HAVE YOU FORGIVEN THEM OR NAH?

----

warm,
loved &
sexy.

Feeling of the day: ------------   Date: ------------

Date: _____

_____
_____
_____
_____
_____

you are the

shit!

feeling of the day: _____

_____
_____
_____
_____
_____
_____
_____
_____

"YOUR PAIN CAN BE THE RESULT OF SOMEONE'S PAIN. TRAUMA & HURT ARE REVOLVING DOORS. AT SOME POINT, IT WILL BE YOUR TURN. OWN IT."

SHARDE' O.

Date: _____

feeling of the day: _____

JUST A LIL'
razzle dazzle

SAFE!!

SAFE!!

SAFE!!

Feeling of the day: ------------   Date: ------------

WEEKLY GRATITUDE NUDGE

TODAY I'M THANKFUL FOR:

TODAY I'LL ACCOMPLISH:

NOTES:

CHALLENGE OF THE WEEK

Do one of the activities on your bucket list.

"

Even when you pour your heart out, it doesn't mean the listener will receive and respond to it in the way you desire. Stick in there, use your voice, do it for you, not for them.

-
Sharde'O.

WRITE A SONG ABOUT YOUR LIFE IN ITS CURRENT ~~STATE~~ *state*

REMINDER

Dear self, don't be insecure. You're exactly who and where your supposed to be .

Write about how that statement on the previous page made you feel.

feeling of the day: ------

Date: ------

HOBBIES

Stuff I am going to try:

Acceptance Shit

WHAT HAVE YOU STRUGGLED WITH ACCEPTING IN YOUR LIFE AND/OR YOUR RELATIONSHIPS? WHAT HAS KEPT YOU FROM DOING SO?

IT'S
UP

Feeling of the day: _____   Date: _____

Feeling of the day: -----------

Date: -----------

Always remember why you started.

Feeling of the day: _____   Date: _____

Date:

Feeling of the day:

LOVE
you more than your
desire to please others

WEEKLY PISTIVITY PURGE

TODAY I'M PISSED ABOUT:

TODAY I'LL RESOLVE THIS BY:

NOTES:

PRACTICE OF THE WEEK

Write five affirmations and say them outloud for five days this week.

"Criticism is not about you; however, consider the benefit of others' perspectives."

Sharde' O.

WHAT MAKES YOUR ENVIRONMENT A *vibe*

REMINDER

Dear self, forgiveness is for you. Focus on your desire to be whole and not on the person who is responsible for testing your commitment to that.

Write about how that statement on the previous page made you feel.

Date: - - - - - - - - -

feeling of the day: - - - - - - - - -

Make them
happen by: _____

DREAM LIST

My Dreams:

Self-Control Shit

WHAT PEOPLE/PLACES/FEELINGS MAKE IT HARD FOR YOU TO USE SELF-CONTROL? HOW CAN YOU MAKE MOMENT-BY-MOMENT CHOICES TO PRACTICE SELF-CONTROL?

----

tuh

[not going + really doe]

Feeling of the day: _____   Date: _____

Prepare

FOR SUCCESS

SO IT'S NOT A

SURPRISE

Feeling of the day: _____   Date: _____

So boundaries. Setting them. Keeping them. And holding folks accountable. How is that working for you?

Date:

Feeling of the day:

Bruh

YOU ARE THE BIG DEAL

Find your **SEXY**

Feeling of the day: ------------   **Date:** ------------

WEEKLY GRATITUDE REMINDER

TODAY I'M THANKFUL FOR:

TODAY I'LL ACCOMPLISH:

NOTES:

HOMEWORK FOR THE WEEK

Write a letter to the future you and mail it to yourself. Schedule opening it five years from now. This letter should include goals, interpersonal struggles you want to move past, people you need to shed, and dreams you need to make space in reality for. The purpose is manifesting your destiny.

TRY NEW WAYS TO LIVE

LET'S GET SKRAIGHT TO IT ... WHO ARE YOU SIS? COMPARE THAT TO WHO YOU WANT TO BE?

DATE:

REMINDER

Dear self, love is a feeling. It isn't enough to maintain a relationship. Be clear about your needs and what the other person is offering.

Write about how that statement on the previous page made you feel.

feeling of the day: ----------

date: ----------

To get by: _____

WISH LIST

I will manifest these things:

Skraighten Shit

WHAT ABOUT YOUR LIFE DO YOU NEED TO GET CLEAR ? WHAT EXPERIENCES DO YOU NEED TO PROCESS OR STOP AVOIDING?

STOP SLEEPIN' ON

ME

Feeling of the day: _____   Date: _____

Feeling of the day: ------

Date: ------

"

Sometimes even when people do their best, it still may not be enough. It's ok. Be clear about what you need and what you are responsible for.

-
Sharde'O.

baddie

a funky, fresh, fly ass woman on top of her business, responsible, loving, sexy, unique, owner of her body, women of her word, communicative, delicate, vulnerable, A-FUCKING-MAZING.

Feeling of the day: ------------ **Date:** ------------

fly guy

a bomb ass, fresh to death, man of his word, accountable, reliable, considerate, thoughtful, loving, sexy, owner of his manhood, manager of his pride, innovative, communicative, well-rounded and A-FUCKING-MAZING.

WHERE THERE IS A WILL

VIGILANT

YOU MAKE YOUR WAY

Feeling of the day: ------------   **Date:** ------------

WEEKLY PISTIVITY PURGE

TODAY I'M PISSED ABOUT:

TODAY I WILL RESOLVE THIS BY:

NOTES:

CHALLENGE FOR THE WEEK

Plant a seed and grow it as a representation of your journey and continued growth.

"A FLOWER
DOES NOT THINK OF
COMPETING WITH
THE FLOWER NEXT TO IT.
IT JUST BLOOMS."

UNKNOWN

HOW ARE YOU TAKING CARE OF YOUR PHYSICAL HEALTH? WHEN IS THE LAST TIME YOU SAW YOUR DOCOTR? WHAT ARE YOUR BODY GOALS?

Feeling of the day: _____   Date: _____

REMINDER

Dear self, boundaries are not optional; they're required. Co-dependency is not healthy and doesn't facilitate speaking and living your truth because your too busy living a life that isn't yours.

Write about how that statement on the previous page made you feel.

Date: - - - - - - -

Feeling of the day: - - - - - - -

To do by: ______________

FOCUS LIST

Things I will to focus on:

Broken Shit

WHAT BEHAVIORS DO YOU STRUGGLE WITH AS A RESULT OF YOUR HURT OR TRAUMA? HOW DO YOU CONTINUE TO LIVE OUT THAT STORY?

You are your future

HOW DOES THE STORY READ?

Feeling of the day: ------------   Date: ------------

LOVE YOU DOWN

"

Time is your constant reminder that your end is inevitable. Be present. Focus on now.

-
Sharde'O.

vibe

[you + fiya shit]

Feeling of the day: ------------   **Date:** ------------

YOU ARE

more than a

NOTION

Feeling of the day: ------------   Date: ------------

WEEKLY GRATITUDE NUDGE

TODAY I'M THANKFUL FOR:

TODAY I'LL ACCOMPLISH:

NOTES:

HOMEWORK FOR THE WEEK

Create your self-care plan. Schedule it in your routine for the week.

"TELL YOUR TRUTH. YOU CAN CHOOSE TO LIVE NOW AND DIE LATER."

SHARDE' O.

What stops you from meeting your needs?

REMINDER

Dear self, invest your time in being your best. You are the most expensive thing you own.

Write about how that statement on the previous page made you feel.

Date: - - - - - - - -

Feeling of the day: - - - - - - - -

To do by: ______________

TO GET LIST

Things I will get this year:

WHAT DO YOU HAVE TO BE HAPPY ABOUT? WHAT DO YOU
HAVE TO BE THANKFUL FOR?

Real Love

FEELS BOTH AMAZING & PAINFUL

Date: ----------

Feeling of the day: ----------

Maybe, just maybe,

YOU CAN
BE HAPPY.

It's all subjective.

Feeling of the day: _____   **Date:** _____

24/7 Open

About enduring. How do you endure? How did you build resilience?

SENDING LIGHT AND LOVE

Be intentional
about meeting
your needs

YOUR
INSIDE IS
JUST AS IMPORTANT AS YOUR OUTSIDE

Feeling of the day: _____   Date: _____

WEEKLY PISTIVITY PURGE

TODAY I'M PISSED ABOUT:

_____

TODAY I WILL RESOLVE THIS BY:

_____

NOTES:

CHALLENGE OF THE WEEK

Spend a day outdoors. Plan it. Schedule it. Do it.

"

Finding and living in your awesomeness is a choice, not a default. You can choose to live in your truth or your truth will challenge the existence you choose.

-
Sharde'O.

LABEL YOUR SHIT : RATE YOUR BODY PARTS. RESEARCH WHAT YOU CAN DO TO IMPROVE THOSE PARTS AND LIST THEM OUT.

REMINDER

Dear self, find a safe space to be free and uninhibited. Dance, sing, scream, cry, laugh, sigh, be naked, be merry, be open.

Write about how that statement on the previous page made you feel.

Date: - - - - - - - -

Feeling of the day: - - - - - - - -

To do by date: _____

TO SAY LIST

People you will say your piece to:

WHAT DO YOU DO TO ENSURE YOU HAVE PEACE? HOW HAVE
YOU CREATED A PEACEFUL SPACE IN YOUR HOME?

35%

\+ fear   \= 100%

65%   real shit

resilience

Feeling of the day: _____   **Date:** _____

BE YOUR OWN

PLEASANT

SURPRISE

Feeling of the day: _____   Date: _____

THE YEAR OF
ENDLESS
Opportunity

Write about what your going to do to practice taking advantage of opportunities that will present themselves

WILL YOU PUT YOU

first?

Feeling of the day: ------------   Date: ------------

Date:

feeling of the day:

Stay Fearless

WEEKLY GRATITUDE NUDGE

TODAY I'M THANKFUL FOR:

TODAY I'LL ACCOMPLISH:

NOTES:

PRACTICE OF THE WEEK

Acknowledge and validate one person everyday this week.

"LOVE CANNOT SAVE YOU.
YOU ARE RESPONSIBLE
FOR SAVING YOURSELF.
YOUR LIFE DEPENDS ON IT."

SHARDE' O.

WHAT ARE HAPPY
FEELINGS? HOW DO YOU
KNOW IF YOUR
SKRAIGHT OR NOT?

REMINDER

Dear self, you are the future. You are the past. You are everything you think you are. So check that shit.

Write about how that statement on the previous page made you feel.

Date: - - - - - - - - -

feeling of the day: - - - - - - - - -

SIS ... WHAT WE DOIN' THIS WEEK ?

TASK	S	M	T	W	T	F	S
_____	○	○	○	○	○	○	○
_____	○	○	○	○	○	○	○
_____	○	○	○	○	○	○	○
_____	○	○	○	○	○	○	○
_____	○	○	○	○	○	○	○
_____	○	○	○	○	○	○	○
_____	○	○	○	○	○	○	○
_____	○	○	○	○	○	○	○
_____	○	○	○	○	○	○	○
_____	○	○	○	○	○	○	○
_____	○	○	○	○	○	○	○
_____	○	○	○	○	○	○	○

NOTES

WHAT IS YOUR PURPOSE? WHY DO YOU WAKE UP EVERY MORNING? OUTSIDE OF YOUR RESPONSIBILITIES, WHAT IS JUST FOR YOU?

feeling of the day: -------------

Date: -------------

BRAVE

CUTE

Feeling of the day: _____   Date: _____

Be clear about who you are, so you don't give someone else the power to define you.

LOOK FOR THE
THE
love

feeling of the day:

feeling of the day: ----------

Date: ----------

giving very much ...

DAILY GRATITUDE REMINDER

TODAY I'M THANKFUL FOR:

_____

TODAY I'LL ACCOMPLISH:

_____

NOTES:

CHALLENGE FOR THE WEEK

Identify, create and communicate one boundary with someone or something.

Needs & wants are two different things. Be clear about the difference.

-

Sharde'O.

ARE YOU A WORKER OR AN ENTREPRENEUR?

(Either is great. You just need to know which fits you.)

REMINDER

Dear self, on this journey, be kind to me. You will make mistakes, you will struggle, you will do your best. Be patient.

Write about how that statement on the previous page made you feel.

feeling of the day: ----------

Date: ------------

Budget Shenanigans

MONTH: YEAR:

SOURCE	DESCRIPTION	AMOUNT	DUE DATE	NOTES

WHAT ARE YOU PLANNING TO DO ABOUT THE THINGS THAT AREN'T WORKING? HOW WILL YOU CHANGE THE PATTERNS THAT AREN'T SERVING YOU.

feeling of the day: -------------

Date: -------------

FREE
GAME

MEDITATE

Feeling of the day: ------------   Date: ------------

24/7 Open

Dreams live forever. What dreams have you given up on but need to revisit?

_____
_____
_____
_____
_____
_____
_____
_____
_____
_____
_____
_____
_____
_____
_____
_____
_____
_____
_____
_____
_____
_____
_____
_____
_____

ENDURE

Feeling of the day: _ _ _ _ _ _ _ _ _ _ _   Date: _ _ _ _ _ _ _ _ _ _ _

Feeling of the day: ------------   Date: ------------

DAILY GRATITUDE REMINDER

TODAY I'M THANKFUL FOR:

_____

TODAY I'LL ACCOMPLISH:

_____

NOTES:

HOMEWORK FOR THE WEEK

Take yourself on a date. Little phone. Lots of love.

"

The experience is only as harmful as you value it.

-

Sharde'O.

WHAT HAVE YOU LEARNED FROM AN EX?

REMINDER

Dear self, you are resilient. Use that to encourage you through the hills and valleys. The journey is just that.

Write about how that statement on the previous page made you feel.

Date: - - - - - - -

Feeling of the day: - - - - - - -

SIS ... WHAT WE DOIN' THIS WEEK?

TASK	S	M	T	W	T	F	S
_____	◯	◯	◯	◯	◯	◯	◯
_____	◯	◯	◯	◯	◯	◯	◯
_____	◯	◯	◯	◯	◯	◯	◯
_____	◯	◯	◯	◯	◯	◯	◯
_____	◯	◯	◯	◯	◯	◯	◯
_____	◯	◯	◯	◯	◯	◯	◯
_____	◯	◯	◯	◯	◯	◯	◯
_____	◯	◯	◯	◯	◯	◯	◯
_____	◯	◯	◯	◯	◯	◯	◯
_____	◯	◯	◯	◯	◯	◯	◯
_____	◯	◯	◯	◯	◯	◯	◯
_____	◯	◯	◯	◯	◯	◯	◯
_____	◯	◯	◯	◯	◯	◯	◯

NOTES

Get that Shit

HOW HAVE YOU MADE FRIENDS? DO YOU NEED TO MAKE NEW FRIENDS?

TURN UP

----

proud

Feeling of the day: ------------   Date: ------------

2017 Open

you can agree to disagree but will you? Can you accept someones perception of you that you don't agree with?

Date: _____

feeling of the day: _____

MODEL

who you want to be

----

hugs +
kisses

CONNECTION & LANGUAGE OF LOVE

Feeling of the day: ------------   **Date:** ------------

Date:

Feeling of the day:

My Boo

Since Forever

DAILY GRATITUDE REMINDER

TODAY I'M THANKFUL FOR:

_____

TODAY I'LL ACCOMPLISH:

_____

NOTES:

CHALLENGE OF THE WEEK

ALLOW SOMEONE TO SUPPORT YOU.

ACT OUT YOUR DREAMS

A reminder from the author

Congratulations on completing this journey and prioritizing yourself. I want to validate your effort and authenticity. The journey doesn't stop here. Be sure to continue your growth. Water your seed. Look up and look forward. Your life is ahead.

With Joy

Continue your journey
with these spicy items ...

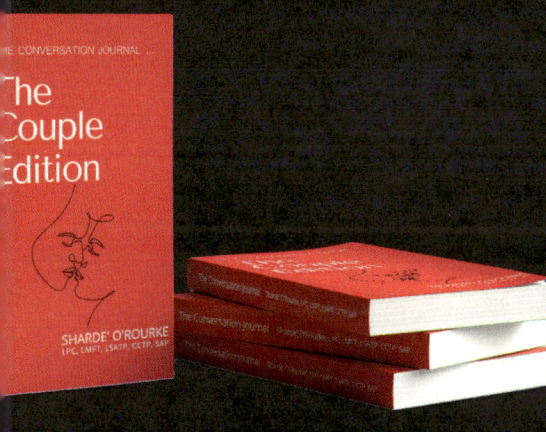

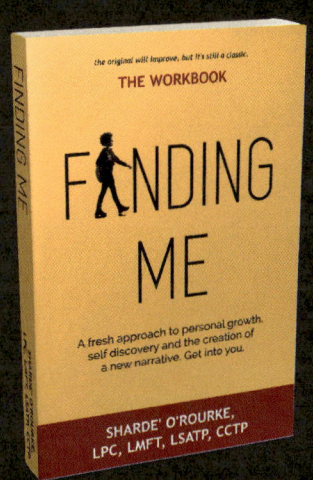